THE FAMILY B

WORD OF THE DAY. FOR A YEAR. EVERY YEAR FOREVER.

JOHNNY PEARCE

The Family Book of Word of the Day. For a Year. Every Year. Forever.

Published by Ginger Prince Publications

Cover design: GPP, attribution to wordclouds.com.

Trade paperback ISBN: 978-0-9935102-7-4

GPP 05/29

Introduction

Vocabulary is more important than you think. Indeed, the number of words children know is a strong predictor of a range of outcomes. The more words a child knows early in their lives, the better they will do in terms of literacy later on, and the better they will do in terms of several other outcomes. And it's not just the number of words, but the quality, too, that can affect these outcomes.

With this in mind, this book intends to give the reader another tool to be able to increase the size of their vocabulary to help you improve your outcome, no matter what your age. And, let's face it, it can be fun to learn new things. Including words!

For each day of the year, there will be a word for you, dear reader, to get to know. You may already know the word, of course. In which case, this is more of a reacquaintance, a chance to get to know each other again. If you are meeting for the very first time, let the friendship blossom. Try and use the word, throughout the day, in a conversation or an email. Impress your teacher, or your boss, with your newfound lexical proficiency.

Within the book, there will be three types of words: nouns (n.), adjectives (adj.) and verbs (v.). Each definition will be very simple after telling you what type of word it is. After this, I add a comment. Just for fun. Because looking at words endlessly can be a bit dry. These comments can be points of interest, expansions of examples, or just drivel that can be ignored. It's up to you.

Any word with * next to it features elsewhere in the book. I have also tried hard not to include any word as a main word that has variant spellings in the UK and US, though I couldn't help it in my definitions and comments.

Challenge yourself to use these words as much as you can. If people look at you strangely, look right back at them even more strangely.

Acknowledgements

Of course, it would be remiss of me not to show huge appreciation to Collins online dictionary and the Online Etymology Dictionary: both have been invaluable in compiling this book. Etymology, as the study of the history of words, is a fascinating area full of interest that reflects history as a whole.

I have also dipped into many other online dictionaries and repositories of words, including (but in no way limited to) Merriam-Webster, thesaurus.com and wordthink.com.

For any word here, or any word you, the reader, comes across, I advise you to look it up, to find out its etymology. All of this added information helps you to remember the word, to feel comfortable with it, and make you far more likely to use it. Words are to play with; be playful.

Massive thanks to the great Donna Tatem for checking over the book. I hope she learnt some new words. I know I did…

This book is dedicated to wordsmiths
and wordaholics
the world over.

ubiquitous

adj. – being present, everywhere

Smartphones are now so ubiquitous that it's odd when someone doesn't have one.

Some might say this isn't a good thing. Apart from when you want to Google the meaning of an unknown word.

cornucopia

n. – a large number of different things

There was a cornucopia of different foods on the table.

From Latin, meaning "horn of plenty", the "-copia" part from which we also get "copious", though this is not a word I have included in this copious range of words.

melancholy

n. – an intense feeling of sadness

The picture he painted of the mourners at the funeral was filled with great melancholy.

This word has very little to do with melons. I usually associate this fruit with happiness and sunshine.

synergy

n. – the potential ability of individuals or groups to be successful by working together

There was a synergy between the two groups of scouts that meant they built their camp more quickly.

Originally from the Greek: "syn" = "together"; "ergon" = "work".

blarney

n. – flattering talk used to coax*, cajole* or wheedle*

"I think you're such a good cook, certainly the best I've ever known. Do you fancy cooking tonight?"
"What a load of blarney. Let's get a takeaway."

Kissing the Blarney Stone in Ireland apparently gives the kisser the skill of the "gift of the gab" – a great skill of flattery.

quintessential

adj. – the most perfect or typical example of something

A good cup of tea is a quintessentially British thing.

As is queuing for things, fish and chips, and crumpets, apparently. But not pandas. Or alligators.

disabuse

v. – to persuade someone that what they believe is untrue

"You're rubbish at football."
Jim disabused Harry of the notion that he was a good footballer.

Please don't disabuse me of the belief that compiling this book was worthwhile by giving it a bad review. I'll cry.

rectitude

n. – quality or attitude of honesty or good moral correctness

The headteacher of the school was someone of great moral rectitude.

A *rect*angle has right angles. Fun fact: squares are a type of (regular) rectangle. Oblongs are what people generally mean by rectangle.

transhumanism

n. – the use of technology to allow humans to be capable of more than they naturally would

Using transhumanist technology, Mr Smith turned himself into a cyborg and lived for 436 years.

There is a strong chance you might get bored if you lived forever. What do you think? Would you want to live for *that* long?

symbiotic

adj. – of a relationship where organisms or people live together to the benefit of both.

Bees and flowering plants have a symbiotic relationship – they each benefit from the other.

Symbiosis comes from the Greek words meaning "with" and "living". There are three types of symbiosis in biology. Ah, but what are they?

disingenuous

n. – when something said is insincere, deceptive or misleading on purpose

"Miss, the dog ate my homework."
"This is a disingenuous attempt to take advantage of my kindness."

It means "not ingenuous", "not noble" or "not innocent". "Honest", "frank" or "trustworthy" are antonyms (opposites).

stipulate

v. – to specify that something must be done

Ari stipulated what the rules of the game were and that the other children should adhere to them.

I am stipulating that you must read one of these words every single day for a year. Without exception.

trenchant

adj. – clear, effective and forceful, usually for a comment or criticism.

Ana was upset with the trenchant criticism of her writing.

Mind you, she didn't use any capital letters or full stops (periods), so she had it coming.

elixir

n. – a liquid considered to have magical powers

The wizard drank the elixir in the hope that it would make him as strong as an ox. It didn't.

Sometimes things just disappoint us. Oh well, better luck with the next elixir.

vicarious

adj. – to get a feeling of doing something without actually doing it, usually by watching or listening to someone else

His granddad, who used to play himself, got vicarious enjoyment of the tennis by watching his grandson play every week.

The sense underlying "vicar" is "substitute" or "one acting in place of another"; the Latin "vicarius" means "substitute".

dauntless

adj. – brave, confident, not easily frightened

The soldiers carried on, dauntless, despite their losses.

I also like "undaunted" as a word. Don't be daunted, use them both. And "daunted". In fact, use all three today. It's a dare.

hirsute

adj.- hairy

The man was very hirsute, with long shaggy hair, a beard, and even a hairy back.

It could be the shortest definition in the book. But you'd have to read them all to find out.

euphoria

n. – a feeling of intense happiness or excitement

A sense of euphoria swept over Mo as he finished his homework.

It's just like the euphoria you get when you finish a book. How far to go? ONLY JANUARY 18TH!!

circumscribe

v. – to restrict the limits of something or draw a line around something

After scoring a goal, he circumscribed his emotions so the other team wouldn't feel so bad.

Task: I stipulate* that you draw a circle around a square. Finished? You've now circumscribed the square. Well done.

haggard

adj. – a tired, gaunt look

After returning from the expedition, the explorer looked haggard.

As am I, when I eventually finish writing a book. Too many late nights. Comes from the older French word meaning "untamed hawk". Different from being "hawkish", though.

mellifluous

adj. – smooth, pleasing (sound)

The notes from the instrument floated mellifluously in the air.

I wrote a book with another author once, about the Maya. He used this word. I had to look it up. I'm not saying he's more verbose than me, though…

kowtow

v. – to bend to the will of someone else, showing them respect

The king's servants would kowtow to him when in his presence and then mock him when he had gone.

It also means to kneel and touch the ground with your forehead and comes from the Chinese meaning "bump head".

caustic

adj. – capable of burning or corroding by a chemical reaction;
sarcastic and cutting

*Caustic substances can dissolve other substances; they are harsh but not
as caustic as your wit.*

Pure caustic soda, or lye, is used to make candles and soap.
Impure caustic soda is used to make drain cleaner.

lackadaisical

adj. – lay or idle

*Greta had a very lackadaisical outlook on life. She likes to let life happen
to her.*

Some people pronounce this word as though it has an "s" after
"lack". Perhaps it's a mix up with the word "lax". I suppose as
long as people understand you, it doesn't matter! Discuss.

phantasm

n. – phantom, ghost

He thought he saw a ghost, a phantasm, but it was just a trick of the mind.

A cool word but not nearly as cool as "phantasmagorical". Infinitely cooler.

fecund

adj. – fertile, productive

The farmland was fecund, producing bumper crops every year.

From the Latin "fecundus" meaning "fruitful". Would a fruit bowl be fecund because it's often full of fruit?

clarion

n. – a type of trumpet; adj. – clear, ringing, inspiring

The final whistle was a clarion call to the fans to run on the pitch.

The instrument "clarinet" has also been written as "clarionet", with "clarion" and "clarinet" having similar histories.

satiate

v. – to fill or satisfy in terms of food or desires

Two hours at the amusement arcade was enough to satiate Jessica's desire to play video games.

While it has generally meant to satisfy one's desires, it now often means to have *too* much of a good thing. Yes, you can have too many cookies. Fact.

ethereal

adj. – delicate, exquisite; spiritual or not of the world of matter

The mist glowed an eerie, ethereal green.

From the Latin "aether" meaning "the upper pure, bright air; sky" etc. What may or may not exist in the aether, out there, that you can't touch? Your mind? Or is that in your brain?

sporadic

adj. – occurring at irregular intervals

The thunder shook sporadically in the near distance.

Comes from the Greek for "scattered", which comes from "spora" meaning "a sowing" (seeds). Which will be where we get "spores" from, that are the little "seeds" that mushrooms scatter when they want more, little mushrooms!

irascible

adj. – easy to anger

I didn't get any sleep last night and I am hungry, so I am very irascible right now. Don't annoy me.

I have twin boys who get very hangry – hungry and angry. This is textbook irascibility. Ooh, nice word.

churlish

adj. – rude, unpleasant, bad-tempered

It would be churlish of me not to offer you a cup of tea.

As we have seen, this is the quintessence* of being British. If tea is not your thing, what would it be churlish of if you didn't offer it to an unannounced guest?

ostentatious

adj. – pretension, showy, over-the-top in trying to impress others

He has a flashy car, a mansion, a yacht. What an ostentatious display of wealth!

Task: See how many people you meet or come across today who are displaying ostentatious behaviour. Mentally record it.

cogent

adj. – compelling, reasonable and forceful (argument or belief)

There are some really cogent arguments against children having mobile phones.

Yeah, but try convincing your children of them…

flounce

v. – to move in exaggerated ways to show you are upset or annoyed, or just to attract attention

Peter flounced out of the room in a right old huff.

Perhaps from the Norwegian "flunsa" meaning "to hurry, work hurriedly", but the English usage was first recorded 200 years before the first Norwegian usage. So who knows?

ineffable

adj. – too great to be described in words

She had such ineffable beauty that words failed me.

I remember singing this word in a hymn at school. Now I know what it means. From the Latin "unutterable".

volition

n. – power and will to do something yourself

Maya did that of her own volition. She's to blame!

Do we have free will? Hmmm. Or were you always going to do that, at that time, and in that place, being who you are? More hmmm. Discuss.

higgledy-piggledy

adj. – disorganised, jumbled, muddled

Finn's lines were drawn higgledy-piggledy across his page.

Careless Finn.
See pell-mell*.

regale

v. – to give delight or amusement to

As they sat around the campfire, Oscar regaled his friends with stories of his expedition.

Comes from the French "gale", meaning "joy". The prefix "re" means again.

ephemeral

adj. – lasts for only a short time or one day

The beautiful chalk picture was, alas, ephemeral, giving way to the heavy rains later that day.

But at least it wasn't graffiti, eh! Or was it? When does pavement art become graffiti and vice versa?

commemorate

v. – to remember an important event with a special action or ceremony

They commemorated winning the cup by having a parade around the city.

I don't like to commemorate my birthday; it makes me feel old.

fraught

adj. – filled or charged with; showing tension or worry

Because the mission was fraught with danger, Max looked fraught.

A double-whammy for you there. What are the most times you can use a word in a sentence where the word has a different meaning each time?

faze

v. – to worry, disturb or shock

Jill was not fazed by the loud explosion next to her house.

That's what happens when you're reading a really good book. With lots of words in.

plethora

n. – an excess, a large amount of something, an overabundance

There was a plethora of reasons not to go into the spooky house.

But because Roberto was dauntless*, and he was sure there would be no phantasms* about, he went in anyway.

gregarious

adj. – outgoing, friendly, social

Arif was a really gregarious guy, very popular at parties.

Antonyms: unsocial, ungregarious, solitary, cespitose, nonsocial, shy. Wow, I've never even *seen* the word "cespitose" before.

pensive

adj. – thoughtful

Scratching his chin, Michael was quiet and pensive.

In the Harry Potter books, a Pensieve is a magical object used to extract thoughts and memories from the person using it. I need to use one every day to locate my car keys.

caprice

n. – sudden, unpredictable change in attitude, a whim

Her decision not to go to the party was mere caprice; she had no real reason but just decided on a whim to stay at home.

I like the word "capricious". The etymology (word history) of caprice is unknown but might have something to do with goats and hedgehogs. Apparently.

nebulous

adj. – vague, lacking definite form

His plan to take over the world was nebulous, lacking in any detail. He failed.

Comes from the Latin "nebulosus" meaning "cloudy, misty, foggy". The cloud type cirrostratus nebulosus has the appearance of a veil covering the sky. It's broadly featureless.

visceral

adj. – instinctive, emotional, intuitive, rather than intellectual

Armando had a visceral dislike of the idea of riding on a horse.

I wonder who the first person to ride a horse was. I bet that took some guts.

odious

adj. – offensive, repugnant*

Vanessa thought that Gerald was a repugnant little man.

Ooh, she sounds upset with him. Perhaps it's a visceral* reaction.

altruism

n. – unselfish concern for others

Gareth gave some money to charity in a fit of altruism.

This raises the age-old question: is there such a thing as altruism? Did Gareth do it subconsciously to make himself feel better? To look good to others? Hmmm. Discuss.

pell-mell

adj. – in a disorderly, confused manner

The horses thundered pell-mell towards the gate.

It has been seen as "pelly melly" in 15th century English. Let's bring it back!

bucolic

adj. – rural, of the countryside, rustic

The landscape in front of them was a bucolic paradise.

Ancient Greek bucolic poetry, written by people like Theocritus, was, I assume, poems written about the countryside. And farms. And shepherds. And shepherds on farms in the countryside.

nefarious

adj. – villainous, wicked

The nefarious ne'er-do-well* was up to no good in the village.

Nefarious is another word I like. It is kind of onomatopoeic. Is it odd to like words? What are your top three words?

pugnacious

adj. – ready for a fight, combative

The village innkeeper was a pugnacious man who wasn't afraid to throw people out of his establishment.

Other synonyms: belligerent*, antagonistic, bellicose*, quarrelsome, truculent*, brawling, disputatious.

antiquated

adj. – old, ancient; old-fashioned, outmoded

The antiquated grandfather clock stood there in the corner of the village mayor's house, gathering dust.

Some of these words in this book might be seen to be antiquated (obsolete, even). Let's reverse that trend.

tedious

adj. – tiresome, boring, monotonous

Talking to the village butcher was a tedious affair, as he droned on and on about meat. You couldn't get a word in edgeways.

Some people think finding out definitions of words is tedious. Not me. No, siree. It's not tedious like a Sisyphean* task. You'll have to wait for that one…

February 27ᵗʰ

voluminous

adj. – of great size, quantity or volume

The village hall was voluminous and echoes bounced off the bare walls.

There's an awful lot going on in this village, isn't there? Voluminously so.

sanguine

adj. – cheerful, confident, optimistic; blood-red

The barman at the village inn was sanguine, both in manner and in looks.

Originally from the Latin "sanguineus" meaning "of blood," and "bloody, bloodthirsty".

bounteous

adj. – giving freely, generous, plentiful, abundant

The village farm had a bounteous supply of wheat for the villagers due to the kindness of the farmer.

Gosh, this village really is the gift that keeps on giving. Some might say it is…bounteous.

intermittent

adj. – happening occasionally or at irregular intervals, off and on

The light from the ship flashed intermittently for several hours.

Related to "intermission" ("inter" = between, "mittere" = "let go, send").

placate

v. – stop someone from being angry

David placated his friend, Ali, who was very angry at being left out of the team, calming him with kind words.

This comes from the Latin "placare" meaning "to please", which is also, through a strangled path, where we get "please" from.

myopic

adj. – short-sighted (both in terms of sight and thought)

Daisy had such myopic opinions about politics. She never really put much thought into it and considered only things that affected her personally.

Eagles can see clearly about eight times as far as humans, spotting a rabbit from two miles. They can also quickly shift focus, allowing them to essentially "zoom" in on their prey.

cerebral

adj. – of the brain; intellectual (rather than emotional)

Even though the play they watched was very cerebral, making them think, it was also very funny.

The human brain can generate 23 watts of power when awake and is 60% fat (one of the fattiest organs in the body), taking 20% of the body's blood and oxygen. How selfish.

frenetic

adj. – fast, frantic, frenzied and other words beginning with f.

The dance routine was frenetic – energetic but also a little chaotic.

From the Greek meaning "frenzy, mental disease, insanity," literally "inflammation of the brain," from "phrēn" being "mind, reason" + "-itis" meaning "inflammation."

placid

adj. – calm, not easily upset or angry

The librarian sat there, placid. She hardly even moved, silently regarding the room.

Plácido Domingo, a famous opera singer, could hardly be seen as placid, midway through belting out an aria.

pernicious

adj. – wicked, harmful, malicious

Those pernicious lies that he was told have greatly undermined his ability to rule the country.

From the Latin: "per" meaning "completely" + "necis" meaning "violent death, murder". Nice. A necromancer is a magician who can supposedly resurrect people.

lucid

adj. – clear, easy to understand

Her account of the events from yesterday were both lucid and accurate.

A lucid dream is one where the dreamer is aware they are dreaming and they may be able to control it slightly. These can be of great interest to dream researchers.

ravenous

adj. – extremely hungry

When she got home, she was so ravenous that she ate all of her food in five minutes flat.

This and "raven" are unrelated. They are homographs (two words spelled alike but with different meanings or derivations – etymologies) by coincidence.

nascent

adj. – just beginning or just being born

His nascent plan to take over the world needed a lot more…thought.

A baby human is born with more bones – a total of some 300 – than the adult they will grow into. Some of these bones fuse together so that only 206 are left.

enigmatic

adj. – mysterious, puzzling

Jennifer was a very enigmatic person; I could never work her out or predict what she would do.

Facebook fact: With 70 likes, it knows/predicts you better than a friend; with 150 likes, better than a family member. And with 300 likes, it knows you better than your spouse.

coltish

adj. – playful, lively but ungainly and awkward in movement

The young lad was coltish, his limbs growing longer than he had been able to master.

When baby horses (colts) are born, they are long-limbed and ungainly, finding movement awkward. Some people are like that all their lives. We're all different. Or are we? (See above).

ruminate

v. – to think deeply about something; to bring food up from your stomach to chew it again

Elsie ruminated on the problem she had to solve.

Humans don't ruminate like cows do. When our food goes on to our stomachs, we hope it doesn't go into reverse.

tumultuous

n. – agitated, disturbed, turbulent

The announcement to the room was met with a tumultuous reception by the people inside.

"Orange" famously has no perfect rhymes. I struggle to find a perfect rhyme for tumult or tumultuous (yes, there are "-uous" rhymes, but…).

bellicose

adj. – aggressive, warlike, ready to fight

The country's attitude towards its neighbour was very bellicose.

"Antebellum" means "before the war" ("bellum is Latin for "war"), especially the American Civil War. Antonym: pacific*.

incessant

adj. – not ceasing, continual

The rain was an incessant torrent falling from the dark clouds.

The past participle of "cedere", meaning "to cease", "cesssus" is the root word in many other words: cessation, procession, etc. How many can you think of?

benign

adj. – showing kindness; having favourable conditions

Is there such a thing as a benign dictator?

Well, is there? Or have all dictators been despotic*?

despotic

adj. – using power in an unfair way, like a despot, tyrannical

All dictators seem to be despotic by nature.

Are they? Have all dictators been despotic, or have any been benign*?

audacious

adj. – bold, daring, risk-taking

It was an audacious attempt to storm the ramparts of the castle and it actually paid off.

Audacious sounds a bit like bodacious* but it's not actually related. Same with loquacious*. And fallacious*.

obsequious

adj. – showing too much willingness to obey or serve someone else in what they say

The king's adviser was obsequious in everything he said to his ruler, gaining his trust through flattery.

This is one of those words that has an almost onomatopoeic quality – it almost sounds like the feeling you get from it.

acrid

n. – pungent, sharp in smell or taste

The chemical fire let off a particularly acrid smell that burnt his nose.

Again, there is a sharpness to this word that is almost onomatopoeic. Acrid gets up your nostrils.

serendipity

n. – a gift of luck in having things come to pass or finding things by chance

Sheer serendipity brought me to the shop where I met my childhood friend.

Coined by Horace Walpole (1717-92) in a letter; he said he formed it from the Persian fairy tale "The Three Princes of Serendip," whose heroes "were always making discoveries, by accidents and sagacity, of things they were not in quest of."

histrionic

adj. – dramatic, exaggerated, insincere (behaviour)

After being fouled by an opposing player, Johnson was nothing short of histrionic in the way he rolled around on the pitch as if he'd been shot.

Histrionics is something we definitely see on the fields of certain sports in attempts to hoodwink the referee and curry their favour.

intrinsic

adj. – internal or inherent to its nature

Nature has an intrinsic value that I just can't put my finger on.

Is beauty intrinsic, or does it lie in the eye of the beholder?

apoplectic

adj. – having apoplexy or extreme anger

Having seen his car destroyed by a falling grand piano from above, the man was apoplectic, jumping from foot to foot and waving his arms.

From the Greek "apoplektikos" meaning "disabled by a stroke, crippled, struck dumb, senseless; crippled, palsied".

credulous

adj. – tending to believe something very easily

He was so credulous he actually believed the President was secretly a lizard man in a human costume.

The reptilian conspiracy theory is believed by too many credulous people: according to one survey, 12 million people in the US believed this.

sentient

adj. – conscious, capable of perceiving senses

Landing on the unknown planet, the team wondered whether there would be sentient alien life.

I have been in rooms full of people and still wondered if there was sentient life thercin.

insular

adj. – of or like an island; remote, detached, aloof

Travis led an insular life, not having any friends and rarely leaving the house.

He is a rock, he is an island. So said Simon & Garfunkel.

sycophant

n. – a person who acts obsequiously* to someone to gain for themselves

The political leader had many sycophants around him who would never disagree with anything he said.

I expect you to agree with me here. Sycophantically nodding your head and smiling widely.

incendiary

adj. – capable of catching or causing fire; inflammatory, creating strife

"That was an incendiary thing to have said. They're going mad about it in the meeting."

Incendiary bombs were used by all sides in World War II, intending to burn once they had been dropped, sadly enough.

magnanimous

adj. - generous

He was as magnanimous in victory afterwards as he is always gracious in defeat.

The ancient Greek Democritus stated that "magnanimity consists in enduring tactlessness with mildness".

veracity

adj. – true, accurate; truthfulness

"There is no veracity to your claim. It is bunkum.* Sheer bunkum."

April Fools'.

bunkum

n. – untrue, nonsense

"There is no veracity* to your claim. It is bunkum. Sheer bunkum."

April Fools'. Still.

onerous

adj. – laborious, of a task you dislike doing

Digging the trench was an onerous task.

Remember, I want you to use this word three times today. But don't make the task onerous…

ambivalent

adj. – not bothered either way about something

The author was ambivalent about whether his definition was good enough and moved on quickly to the next word.

I'm ambivalent about whether this sentence is worth writing.

rambunctious

adj. – full of energy and difficult to control

The children were as rambunctious as the puppies next door.

Boisterous is another good word meaning similarly. Raucous and unruly do a good job too. And perhaps tumultuous*.

abysmal

adj. – immeasurably bad

The weather was abysmal for our holiday. Normal holiday weather, then.

Literally meaning "pertaining to an abyss". If you had an expedition into an abyss, it would be both literally and figuratively abysmal.

spurious

adj. – not genuine or real, dodgy

He decided to leave the party for some spurious reasons.

Shame. It was his own party, and they hadn't given him the bumps yet.

tenacious

adj. – stubborn, persistent; holding on firmly

She's a tenacious player, never giving up, chasing the ball for every point.

Antonyms: yielding, weak, surrendering, irresolute.

cavernous

adj. – like a cavern in vast size, darkness

The room was cavernous inside, tall ceiling and distant walls.

Found in 1991 and 2 to 5 million years old, Hang Son Doong (Mountian River Cave) is the largest cave in the world, located right in the heart of Phong Nha-Ke Bang National Park, Vietnam.

rhetorical

adj. – concerned with the effect and style of speaking

Alisha's speech was a rhetorical masterpiece. The audience was rapt.

I love rhetorical questions. I mean, why wouldn't I?

eccentric

adj. – bizarre, irregular, not the norm

He was an eccentric old man, sticking out from the crowd in what he wore, how he carried himself and what he said.

Question: What's the most eccentric thing you have ever done? Tell someone today the story.

temerity

n. – foolish boldness, rashness, audacity

He had the temerity to suggest to his boss that no one appreciated what they had been asked to do.

HMS Temeraire was a Royal Naval ship whose name comes from the French for "reckless", from the Latin "temeritatem": "blind chance, accident; rashness, indiscretion, foolhardiness".

ambidextrous

adj. – able to use both hands expertly

Being ambidextrous, Aaron was a very useful boxer.

There is no ambiguity in my being ambivalent* about being ambidextrous.

ambisinister

adj. – clumsy in both hands

Trevor was ambisinister. He was rubbish at wood carving.

"Sinister" comes from the Latin for "left". Omens seen on the left were seen as bad luck, probably form the dominance of right-handed people. Left-handedness was associated with evil. So, it turns out one of my sisters is evil and so is my dad.

eclectic

adj. – a variety of sources, styles, ideas etc.

There was an eclectic mix of music at the disco. Everyone was happy at some point.

The English poet William Cowper (1731–1800) in "The Task" wrote: "Variety's the very spice of life, That gives it all its flavour." The Greek dramatist Euripides (c.485–c.406 BCE) in his Orestes said more succinctly, "a change is always nice".

apathetic

adj. – indifferent, having or showing little emotion

Sanjay was apathetic about politics, not being bothered which party he could vote for.

Originally more positive in Greek: "freedom from suffering, impassibility, want of sensation".

cathartic

adj. – reliving of emotional tensions through something or another

The author found that writing out words and their definitions was a cathartic experience. He felt destressed.

That's destressed not distressed. But, I have and will experience both in this mission.

truncated

adj. – shortened by having bits or time cut off

His time in charge of the team was severely truncated after losing his first six matches.

A square-based pyramid that has been truncated is called a frustrum. A football/soccer ball is technically a truncated, inflated icosahedron.

repugnant

adj. – distasteful, disgusting, offensive

The smell was repugnant making her gag reflexively.

Our repugnance to death increases in proportion to our consciousness of having lived in vain.
— William Hazlitt

episodic

adj. – divided into episodes; irregular, occasional, sporadic

Jeremy had episodic migraines that had affected him for years.

Here's a word that seems to have contradictory meanings. Episodes on TV seem to be regular, yet its sporadic meaning seems irregular. Hey ho.

antithesis

n. – the exact opposite

His approach to life is the antithesis of mine.

The antithesis of antithesis is equivalence. Meh.

embellish

v. – to add beauty or detail; to adorn

The child was a good writer and embellished her story with figurative language and flourishes of literary fancy.

"Unless you embellish, you can't tell the truth."
— Marty Rubin

guile

n. – cunning, slyness

In trying to work out a deal to suit everybody, Jim had to use all the craft and guile he had to convince everyone.

Guile was a character from the seminal Street Fighter video game series. He was a brawny US Air Force character with a flat-top haircut who was probably as guileless as could be.

gratuitous

adj. – without cause; unnecessary, unjustified

The action movie that they watched had some gratuitous violence that made it unsuitable for the children to watch.

In philosophy, the Problem of Evil is an argument that seeks to work out how seemingly gratuitous suffering can exist in light of an all-loving, -powerful and -knowing god. Discuss.

tempestuous

adj. – like a storm, turbulent

The two had a tempestuous relationship, always arguing.

The Tempest was one of the last plays Shakespeare wrote alone. It is about some shipwrecked members of a boat caught in a magical storm created by the spirit Ariel.

innocuous

adj. – no harmful effects, inoffensive

What seemed like an innocuous comment was actually a veiled threat.

The seemingly innocuous duck-billed platypus is one of the few mammals to lay eggs and one of the few to be venomous. The males can deliver a sting through a pair of spurs on their hind legs that feels like "hundreds of hornet stings".

hubris

n. – arrogance, pride

It was his great hubris that meant he thought he would actually win this one, and win it easily.

Even great men bow before the Sun; it melts hubris into humility.
—Dejan Stojanovic

punctilious

adj. – attentive to detail, especially regarding manners and etiquette

Carolyn was a punctilious host.

I can't think of anything to say about the word punctilious. I really can't. Sorry, April 28th.

avarice

adj. – extreme greed for riches

Fernando's avarice ate away at his soul as all of his dreams glittered with the gold of others.

Poverty wants some things, Luxury many things, Avarice all things.
—Benjamin Franklin

prostrate

adj. – lying face downwards (in submission); helpless; exhausted

Little Benny lay prostrate on the floor as the exhaustion and occasion overcame him.

Not to be confused with prostate.

miserly

adj. – of or like a miser, avaricious*, greedy, stingy

Ebenezer Scrooge was certainly very miserly.

Who is the biggest miser you know? Give them a gift. Be the change you want to see.

myriad

adj. – innumerable, large number of

There were myriad different ways to complete the puzzle.

Some say "myriads of". It really comes down to whether you're using "myriad" as a noun or an adjective. If it's an adjective, then you would say "myriad ways". If it's a noun, you would say "a myriad of gadgets".

furtive

adj. – in stealth, secret or slyness

She gave a furtive glance over to the man sitting opposite.

From the Latin "furtivus" meaning "stolen," from "furtum" "theft, robbery; a stolen thing", itself from "fur" meaning "a thief". I guess that means fur coats are stolen. Off the animals' bodies. Doesn't get my vote.

haughty

adj. – arrogant

She carried herself in a haughty manner, wrapping her fur coat about her shoulders and striding out of the building.

Haughty? Naughty, more like, with that stolen coat. (See yesterday if you don't understand.)

feckless

adj. – feeble, weak, ineffective

He may have been a feckless and incompetent parent, but he did not deserve to be treated like that.

From the word "feck" meaning "value, effect" where the Scottish shortened "effect" to "feck". Lazy speakers.

acrimonious

adj. – sharp, bitter in manner or temper

Jenkins had an acrimonious split from the club at which he had played for a decade.

Ridicule more often settles things more thoroughly and better than acrimony.
—Horace

automaton

n. – robot; a person who acts robotically

If we have no free will, are we not just biological automatons?

Now that's a good question. Are we biological computers, with our brains as the main CPU?

autonomous

adj. – independent of others, able to operate according to
one's own choosing

The roads will soon be full of autonomous, driverless cars.

Nature is always trying to tell us that we are not so superior or
independent or alone or autonomous as we may think.
—Wendell Berry

paucity

n. – dearth, smallness of number, insufficiency

"Unfortunately, there is a paucity of good places to eat around here."

The horror of the Twentieth Century was the size of each new
event, and the paucity of its reverberation.
—Norman Mailer

benevolent

adj. – kind, charitable, friendly

His contribution to the charity event was a benevolent gesture.

Omnibenevolent means "all-loving", like some gods are claimed to be. I tried being this for just a day and I fell short. Just.

affront

n. – a deliberate insult

Not turning up to the party was a real affront to Margaret.

I would like to take you seriously, but to do so would be an affront to your intelligence.
—George Bernard Shaw

seismic

adj. – relating to an earthquake; of enormous proportions

His decision to stop children wearing uniform represented a seismic shift in the way he ran the school.

The Valdivia Earthquake, Chile, in 1960 represented the biggest magnitude earthquake ever recorded, at 9.5 on the Richter Scale. It left 2 million people homeless.

pipette

n. – a slender tube with a rubber end for sucking up small amounts of liquid

Millie put the pipette into the petri dish and removed a small amount of the liquid for further experimentation.

I miss saying pipette (it's a long time since Chemistry lessons) and can't shoehorn it into conversation easily. Good luck using this today. Unless you are a chemistry teacher.

unflappable

adj. – not easily excited; calm

Given that the tidal wave was on the horizon, she was unflappable in her dedication to getting the children to safety.

Originally used in reference to Harold Macmillan, British P.M. 1957-63. (When I am excited, I definitely flap my arms a lot.)

bandy

v. – to throw, strike to and fro; to pass gossip freely

"I've heard that name bandied around a lot."

Now let us bandy words no more... nothing is easier than sharp words, except to wish them unspoken.
— R. D. Blackmore

flak

n. – adverse criticism; anti-aircraft fire

Jenny took a lot of flak for her controversial decision.

I hope you have more cause to use the former definition than the latter. I wouldn't want to wish war on you.

quid pro quo

n. – a reciprocal exchange, something given to get an advantageous return

It was a quid pro quo for them: if their son behaved well, then he would receive extra technology time.

"This for that": this term has become a hot topic in politics with shady deals. Good for vocabulary use though, I guess.

hunker down

v. – crouching down; avoiding things

"You need to hunker down now and get on with your job. You don't need to be any more noticed than necessary."

"I'm gonna hunker down like a jackrabbit in a dust storm."
— US President, Lyndon B. Johnson

bivouac

n. – temporary camp/shelter; v. – to set up such a camp

The Scouts set up a bivouac that night out of resources found around them.

Probably a word from the Thirty Years' War, ultimately from the Swiss/Alsatian word "biwacht" meaning "night guard".

metronome

n. – a device that sets the beat or tempo for a musician

She went to the shop every morning of every day with the timing precision of a metronome.

The device was patented in England in 1815 by German-born Johann Maelzel (1772-1838), who gave it its modern name, incorporating the ideas of a device invented in Amsterdam.

fervent

adj. – intensely passionate, ardent

She was a fervent supporter of human rights.

Who wouldn't be? Sorry, who shouldn't be? From the Latin "ferventem" meaning "boiling, hot, glowing".

garbled

adj. – jubmled, misxed up, unlcear

The author's definition was a garbled mess.

Do you see what I did there?

Clever.

carte blanche

n. – freedom to fulfil your wishes, full permission

"You have carte blanche with this new project to do exactly what you want."

Akin to a blank cheque/check whereby the "white paper" is left to be signed at their discretion.

brackish

adj. – salty or briny water

The brackish well water was pretty much undrinkable.

From the Scottish "brack" meaning "salty". I wonder if their porridge can be called brackish as they like salt in their porridge, eh?

indomitable

adj. – difficult or impossible to defeat

The castle was an indomitable fortress.

The *Indomitus rex* was a made-up dinosaur in the Jurassic Park movie franchise. The *Metlapilcoatlus indomitus* is a venomous pit viper from Central America.

festoon

v. – to decorate with suspended materials

The village hall was festooned with balloons and ribbons.

From the Latin for "celebration, feast", a festoon (n.) is a chain of flowers or ribbons or whatnot. In dentistry, it is the undulating* shape of where the gums meet the teeth, where "festooning" is making this shape for dentures.

belligerent

adj. – ready to fight/argue, hostile, aggressive

Sam was a belligerent young boy, always arguing with everything his parents said.

From the Latin "to wage war"; being a parent is often like waging war. Bedrooms are like battlefields, toys strewn are the casualties of conflict.

gangly

adj. – tall and slightly awkward

Little Tess went to the Halloween party dressed as a spider with gangly legs.

Mark Twain appeared to adapt this from the Scottish "gang" meaning "to walk" or "gangling". "I should have shot that long gangly lubber they called Hank…" Poor Hank.

anachronism

n. – an event or claim that is historically incorrect

The coffee cup left on the period drama movie set was an anachronism.

Chronos was the personification of time in Greek mythology who, with his daughter, the goddess of inevitability, revolved around the primordial world egg and created another egg that contained two gods who gave birth to the other gods.

gnarled

adj. – rough, twisted, having gnarls (a knot on a tree)

The old tree had a gnarled trunk and twisted branches.

"Gnarly, dude" is surfer speak for dangerous in terms of a wave. Or generally cool. Or sweet. Or excellent. But not usually in terms of tree branches and knots.

vacuous

adj. – empty; lacking in ideas, intelligence

His mind vacuous, Cole stared at the whiteboard blankly.

I have taught and spoken to many people who have looked at me vacuously. Is that my fault or theirs, though?

scintilla

n. – a minute or tiny amount

There wasn't even a scintilla of doubt that Raoul had done it.

From the Latin for "spark, glittering speck, atom":
Parva sæpe scintilla contempta magnum excitavit incendium.
A spark neglected has often raised a conflagration.
—Quintus Curtius Rufus

mettle

n. – courage, spirit

He had his mettle tested early in the game by a huge tackle.

I always thought an unmetalled road was spelled in this way.
It's not.

corollary

n. – a consequence or result of something

The corollary of the policy was a huge amount of carbon dioxide produced.

The corollary of writing this book has been late nights, sore eyes and an influx of tea.

unsurpassed

adj. – unparalleled, better than anything of its kind

Her skill on the pitch was unsurpassed by anyone else in her league.

If there was something you could *realistically* choose to do now to be unsurpassed at in the world, to dedicate all of your time and effort to, what would it be?

turgid

adj. – swollen, congested; pompous or excessively embellished

The sluggish river was turgid with sand and silt.

Yet another word that I have always used slightly incorrectly. This project is enlightening. I thought it was "sluggish and boring" exclusively. Language, eh!

paltry

adj. – insignificant or small amount

The poultry had given the farmer a paltry four eggs for his pantry.

These paltry ten words are all I'll say on it.

flotsam

n. – floating wreckage from a ship; worthless objects

Don't let the flotsam and jetsam of life get in your way.

In UK law, "flotsam" are goods floating on the sea as a result of a wreck, and "jetsam" are things cast from a ship in danger of wrecking, later found ashore. "Lagan" is whatever sinks.

obstinate

adj. – headstrong, difficult to change in opinion

Kai was an obstinate boy who stuck stubbornly to his plan.

I am firm. You are obstinate. He is a pig-headed fool. — Katharine Whitehorn

emblematic

adj. – symbolic or representative of something

Kids on their mobile phones all day, every day, is emblematic of modern life.

The red cross is a *symbol* of the International Red Cross and *emblematic* of humanitarian aid.

permeate

v. – to penetrate or spread though

The cold and wet permeated every seam of his clothes, every fibre of his body.

In geology, permeable rocks absorb water and impermeable ones don't. "Un imperméable" is a raincoat, in French.

zephyr

n. – a gentle wind, breeze

The curtains constantly undulated*, caressed by swirling zephyrs.

I've been singing a song with this word in for almost twenty years and have only now found out what it means. Twenty wasted years...

maverick

n. – a person with independent or different views

He was a real maverick in his sport, playing with his own style.

First from 1867 referring to a "calf or yearling found without an owner's brand" from Samuel A. Maverick, a Texas cattle owner who was notoriously negligent in branding his calves. Maverick was maverick. (See also his politician grandson).

incarcerate

v. – to confine or imprison

The trio were incarcerated for ten years each.

Do we incarcerate in order to punish or to rehabilitate? What is more important? How about to deter? Hmmm.
Also, the trio *were* or the trio *was*?

contranym

n. – a word with two opposite meanings

"Literally" is now a contranym because, in dictionaries, it literally means literally as well as non-literally (metaphorically).

This is a ubiquitous* contranym. "He was literally on fire on the soccer pitch!" Was he really? And yet, because they *reflect* language use, some dictionaries now list this definition.

timorous

adj. – timid, weak, overly cautious

Elsie wasn't a timorous woman; she saw herself as gregarious, as a risk-taker, as embracing life.

From the Latin "timere" meaning "to fear", annoyingly close to the Middle English "temerous" meaning "rash" from which we get "temerity"*, an antonym.

escapade

n. – an exciting or dangerous adventure

The superhero had yet another month of daring escapades; having those skills was certainly tiring.

I am trying to think of an example in my life that can be appropriately described as an escapade. Can you?

lampoon

v. – to strongly and humorously criticise someone or something

The newspaper lampooned the school in a harsh article.

This might come from an old French drinking song, of all places, from "lampons", from "lamper" meaning "to drink, guzzle".

dissemble

v. – to conceal by pretence

Ali dissembled his fear by cracking a joke.

I am wondering how I could dissemble my disappointment at still only being on June 18th. Probably not wise to admit it, then.

coax

v. – to persuade or manipulate someone, or something out of someone

James coaxed out of Angel the whereabouts of his best friend.

Nothing to do with coaxing, but June 19th is World Sauntering Day. What a random thing to celebrate, although, in this fast-paced world, a nice saunter is definitely a good thing.

outlandish

adj. – outrageous, odd, peculiar in habits or looks, etc.

Such outlandish behaviour in the palace led to many odd looks and whispers.

No idea is so outlandish that it should not be considered with a searching but at the same time a steady eye.
—Winston Churchill [Not sure about that, Winston…]

untenable

adj. – unable to be held or maintained

Winston's opinion was untenable in light of so many outlandish* ideas.

Take that, Churchill.

diligent

adj. – careful in carrying out a task

Gail diligently went though her ledger, ticking off those who had paid her.

What we ever hope to do with ease, we must first learn to do with diligence.
—Samuel Johnson, who wrote the first dictionary. Diligently.

macabre

adj. – ghastly, grim, gruesome and other g words

The murder scene was a macabre affair, one that he did not want to remember.

Despite my ghoulish reputation, I really have the heart of a small boy. I keep it in a jar on my desk.
—Robert Bloch

lily-livered

adj. – cowardly, timid

"You lily-livered coward! Come out and face me!"

From Shakespeare's Macbeth, a lily being pale, and the liver being the seat of passion and love…oddly.

surfeit

n. – an excessive amount

There was a surfeit of rations left in the warehouse, still boxed up.

"Facere" is the Latin verb "to do", from where the "feit" part comes. "Sur" is the prefix for "over", thus creating "overdo".

impervious

adj. - impermeable*; not able to be influenced by

Alfonso was impervious to the opposition chants, only concentrating on scoring.

The increase in impervious surfaces in dense cities around the world has meant surface run-off from rainwater has become a problem. More grass needed!

bedraggled

adj. – untidy, unkempt, dirty

The bedraggled figure stumbled through the inn door, lank hair dripping with rain.

From the 1570s, with "draggle" meaning "to wet or befoul a garment by allowing it to drag along damp ground or mud".

penultimate

adj. – the last but one

"This is the penultimate turn before the game finishes."

I wonder, given "the ultimate superhero", whether "the penultimate superhero" is the second-best one? Not such a cool title, even though that's a pretty impressive position.

redux

adj. – something brought back, restored or presented in a
new way

*My blog title, "My Life Goals – Redux" represents a newly updated
vision of what I want to achieve.*

I wonder what the next fashion redux will be. Bell-bottom
jeans?

delectation

n. – delight, enjoyment, entertainment

*"And tonight, for your delectation, I present to you, the greatest magician
in the world!"*

Some might say that I am writing this book for my own
delectation. What will you do today for your own delectation?

dainty

adj. – delicate, elegant

Her dainty figure bobbed and spun across the stage.

The silver birch is a dainty lady,
She wears a satin gown;
The elm tree makes the old churchyard shady,
She will not live in town. (Edith Nesbit)

jilted

from v. – to leave or reject a lover

The bride was jilted at the altar, though this was a blessing in disguise.

If you have ever been jilted, my deep condolences.

reiterate

v. – to repeat something

He reiterated the house rules to his children as once was not enough.

He reiterated the house rules to his children as once was not enough.

fawn

v. – to flatter and admire someone to gain their attention

It was sickening to watch him fawn over her, knowing that he was just after her money.

Originally used in Middle English to refer to expressions of delight and even to a dog wagging its tail (early 14th century.).

sodden

adj. – extremely wet, soaked through

He took off his sodden jumper and hung it by the crackling fire.

Originally from the Old English word for "boiled", ironically, since one is usually cold when sodden.

incognito

adj. – in disguise or under an assumed name

He went incognito through the crowd.

There are times I'd like to be incognito, be someplace where I might not stand out.
—Anne Donovan
To be honest, I've never heard of you.

incommunicado

adj. – not willing or able to communicate; secluded or isolated

Without phone or internet, and stuck at home, he was incommunicado for a week.

The first time I ever heard this word was from the prog-rock band Marillion. True story.

fortitude

n. – strength of mind, endurance

She had the fortitude to carry on, the well of strength and resolve to draw from.

Fortitude is the marshal of thought, the armour of the will, and the fort of reason.
—Francis Bacon

white elephant

n. – a venture that is a useless waste of money

After spending so much money on their horse, after losing eight races, it was beginning to look like a white elephant.

Apparently from the King of Siam who gave a white elephant as a gift because it was expensive and a huge effort to maintain.

dilapidated

adj. – broken down, falling into disrepair

The dilapidated building was in need of much love and attention.

Here's another word I love that really sounds like it feels. I don't know if this is an instant thing or a feeling about a word that develops *because* of its meaning.

expedite

v. – to hasten the progress of, speed up

The package was expedited posthaste.

From the Latin "ex" meaning "out" + "pedis" meaning "fetter, chain for the feet".

chilblain

n. – painful swelling on fingers and toes from the cold

Jim, after the game had finished on that cold winter's day, ran in and had a hot shower. His fingers hurt with the resulting chilblains.

Aah, I haven't had chilblains for years, perhaps since childhood. I need to make myself play sports in the snow in nothing but shorts and a jersey and then have a hot shower.

espouse

v. – to support, adopt (an ideal, policy etc.)

He espoused the equal pay of men and women doing the same job.

Common experience shows how much rarer is moral courage than physical bravery. A thousand men will march to the mouth of the cannon where one man will dare espouse an unpopular cause.
—Clarence Darrow

undulating

adj. – moving in waves or having this appearance

The rolling hills formed an undulating vista in front of him.

The up and down of the stresses for the intonation of this word give it the quality of onomatopoeia.

germane

adj. – relevant to the subject at hand

"More germane to our discussion about children is the idea of 'learning'."

The modern sense of "closely connected, relevant" (c. 1600) comes from its use in *Hamlet*: "The phrase would bee more Germaine to the matter: If we could carry Cannon by our sides." German and germane have similar etymology.

respite

n. – a short pause for rest

After a short respite, the shots rang out across the battlefield again.

I would like to offer you a brief respite with some pictures or something. But, unfortunately, it's just more words from hereon in.

gambit

n. – an opening move, comment or manoeuvre

Her opening gambit in the debate was to set out the best argument her opponent would give,

From Latin, via Italian, about the opening move in chess, first used by Ruy Lopez who himself has an opening move named after him.

belfry

n. – the part in a church tower or steeple where the bells are hung

The workmen had a difficult job of fixing scaffolding up to the belfry.

Unless you live next to a church, this isn't going to be a word you can casually shoehorn into a conversation. Task: use belfry in three sensible ways today in conversation or writing.

genial

adj. – cheerful, warm, easy-going character

Frank was a genial fellow, always popular company.

Originally meaning "pertaining to marriage". Not so much in its modern definition (though I'm not saying you don't get warm, cheerful marriages…).

scapegoat

n. – a person made to bear the blame for others

Alice was the scapegoat for the group getting the task wrong.

Shortened from "escape" goat, originally from Jewish mythology. Don't go blaming other people all your lives, kids; take responsibility for your actions!

comprise

v. – to include, contain, consist of

Pandora's Box comprised terrible evils of the world, including sickness and death, though she was told it contained special gifts.

Actually, it was a jar, but there you go. Don't go opening jars, kids. Eat your greens. Say please and thank you. Eat with your mouth closed. Don't drop litter.

wheedle

v. – to persuade, coax* or cajole* by flattery

"Don't think you can wheedle your way into my good books!"

Wow, a second word from the Thirty Years war that English soldiers stole from the German "wedeln", meaning "wag the tail".

divulge

v. – to disclose, make something known

Ciara divulged her friend's deepest secret.

What is the deepest secret you have ever divulged? How do you feel about it now?

cleave

v. – to split, cut, divide, sever

They cleaved a path through the undergrowth.

This is another example of a contranym* since it can also mean "to bind together" or "to adhere to".

mitigate

v. – to make something become less severe

The school use soundproofing in the hall to mitigate the noise produced by the children at lunchtime.

The Latin word "mitigare" means "soften, make tender, ripen, mellow, tame", which sounds a lot nicer.

hoi polloi

n. – the common people

The politician was bored at having to shake so many hands when meeting the hoi polloi.

From the Greek meaning "the many" or "people". There's no point getting all hoity-toity* over the plebs and the riffraff.

abscond

v. – to escape or run away secretly

Jess absconded from school so she didn't have to do double Science.

But science will provide all the answers to all our problems! She could be the key to unlock our future! Or she could go to the shops without permission to buy something.

skulk

v. – to move about or hide, lurking to avoid notice

Gareth skulked about in the shadows like a small mammal in the woods.

I wonder why. What had he done wrong? Obviously some kind of ne'er-do-well*. No one skulks like that unless they're hiding something…

detritus

n. – debris, disintegrated material

"Look at all this detritus on my desk. Who put this rubbish here?"

Originally used geographically for the rocks scraped away by glaciers and left behind. This came from the Latin, meaning "rubbing away".

repertoire

n. – the entire stock of things available; every song, play, piece of work produced by an artist etc.

Fortunately, Fred's piano repertoire comprised* only "Chopsticks" and "Happy Birthday". The show for his parents wouldn't take long.

Do you have a repertoire of jokes? How many can you remember now? Try to tell all your jokes today.

wangle

v. – to manipulate, get or achieve something using illicit methods.

Jane wangled her way back into her mother's good books.

Originally from printing referring to "fake by manipulation" and later popularised by World War I soldiers.

cataclysm

n. – a large scale natural event (flood etc.)

The decision to invade that country was cataclysmic.

Of course, we basically use every word we can metaphorically. The 1931 China floods caused the death of anywhere between 500,000 and 4,000,000 people. In 1815, Mount Tambora erupted to kill 100,000 people and eventually millions more.

cajole

v. – to persuade or coax* by flattery, wheedle*

He cajoled his friend into playing one more game.

Perhaps a blend of Middle French "cageoler" meaning "to chatter like a jay" and Old French "gaioler" meaning "to cage, entice into a cage".

truculent

adj. – defiantly aggressive, obstreperous

The truculent boy refused to do what he was told.

Two for the price of one, today. You have, free of extra charge, "obstreperous". Every day's a school day.

quixotic

adj. – foolishly idealistic; hopeful yet unrealistic

Her campaign to become the country's leader was a little too quixotic.

Shame. There's nothing wrong with setting yourself idealistic goals. Do better. Be better! Here endeth the lesson.

malodorous

adj. – smelling bad, stinky

The room was deeply malodorous, with unwashed clothes lying around and rubbish on the floor.

Sounds like a typical teenager's room.

ne'er-do-well

n. – a person who can't get things done, irresponsible person

Wilson was a well-known ne'er-do-well in the village, hanging around the well and getting up to no good.

First recorded in 1773. This is the same year as the Boston Tea Party and that Captain Cook and his crew were the first people to cross the Antarctic Circle. There was a big earthquake in…?

loquacious

adj. – talkative

The headmistress was a loquacious woman who had a tendency to let her assemblies drag on.

Personally, I'm not loquacious. I'm more of a, how do you say this, direct person who certainly doesn't like to bang on about the same thing over and over again because I like to keep to th

bodacious

adj. – impressive, excellent

"Dude, that was totally bodacious."

U.S. slang, perhaps from "bodyaciously" meaning "bodily, totally" or a blend of "bold" and "audacious". Popularised again by the movie *An Officer and a Gentleman* all the way back in 1982.

precipitate

v. – to hasten the occurrence of, bring about hastily

The rain precipitated the end of their day trip just as they got to the cliff.

One could say that precipitation precipitated the end, whilst at the precipice, if one was to be perspicacious.

panacea

n. – a remedy or cure for all ills

Buying the children tablets was not the panacea their parents thought it was as the tablets caused more problems than they solved.

Technology, eh!

chock-a-block

adj. – extremely full, jammed

The room was chock-a-block with people – rammed to the hilt.

From a nautical origin where the "chock" + "block" meaning "a pulley together with its framework".

erstwhile

adj. – former, of past times

The whole episode left two erstwhile friends not speaking to each other.

After all, my erstwhile dear,
My no longer cherished,
Need we say it was not love,
Just because it perished?   —Edna St. Vincent Milla

mizzle

v. – to rain finely, drizzle

It always seems to mizzle around here.

Both a verb and a noun, a mizzle is halfway between a mist a drizzle.

tantamount

adj. – equivalent in value, force, effect

What he said was tantamount to admitting he was guilty.

Victory attained by violence is tantamount to a defeat for it is momentary.
—Mahatma Gandhi

pacific

adj. – tending to make or conserve peace

He was a very pacific leader, shying away from conflict.

The Pacific Ocean was named so because in 1519, when Magellan sailed into it, he found it calmer than the stormy Atlantic.

halcyon

adj. – calm, peaceful, tranquil

I remember those halcyon days before this place became the bustling nightmare it is today!

From the Greek word for kingfisher; Halcyone, daughter of Aeolus, when widowed, threw herself into the sea and became a kingfisher. I tried it and became a beached whale.

spoonerism

n. – the swapping of initial letters of two words

Mean as custard. (Keen as mustard.)

Named after Rev. William Spooner who supposedly said, "The Lord is a shoving leopard" instead of "The Lord is a loving shepherd."

bonhomie

adj. – good-heartedness, friendliness

He was all smiles and bonhomie, that day.

If your surname is "Goodman", you are evidently a person of such qualities. Or, at least, you say you are, but are you? Really?

Machiavellian

Adj. – cunning, unscrupulous in a usually deceptive and planned manner

She had Machiavellian machinations underway to oust her boss.

Named after Niccolo Machiavelli (1469-1527), a Florentine statesman and author of *Il Principe*, in which he advised rulers to place advantage above doing the right thing.

omnishambles

n. – total disaster and chaos in usually political situations

The three weeks he had in charge of the school turned out to be an omnishambles.

Shambolic, I tell you! Shambolic!

ken

n. – knowledge, understanding

The hows and whys of working a computer were beyond his ken.

If Sue was married to Ken, then if something was beyond her ken, would it be beyond both of them?

mercurial

adj. – changeable, volatile, erratic

Dora had a mercurial nature, always changing her mind and doing things on a whim.

Supposedly the qualities of the god Mercury, and thus those born under the planet Mercury (astrology); this could also be connected to the qualities of quicksilver (mercury).

tub-thumper

n. – rowdy public speaker, one who vociferously* rants

Though the politician was not a tub-thumper, she got things done in her own quiet way.

A "tub" was 17C slang for a "pulpit", so s tub-thumper was someone who banged the pulpit as they emotionally spoke and ranted.

vociferous

adj. – of great energy, noise, vehemence*

The politician was a real tub-thumper, always ranting vociferously whenever he was on television.*

Literally meaning "carrying the voice".

vehement

adj. – having intense feeling, passion; fervent*, impassioned

The tub-thumping politician was vehement in his denial that it was his fault. For anything.*

How good are you at accepting responsibility for things? Room for improvement?

Shangri-la

n. – a faraway heaven, idyllic place

The deserted island they landed on was a veritable Shangri-La.

From the novel *Lost Horizon* (1933) by James Hilton, where he talked of an imaginary valley in the Himalayas. Also a nursing home down the road from me. I doubt it's very heavenly.

ergophobia

n. – an abnormal fear of work

Alisha always had a bad case of ergophobia hitting her on Sunday nights.

Can a fear of work be abnormal?

ufology

n. – the study of UFOs

Dr. Smith was one of the world's foremost ufologists.

They're out there, somewhere. The distances are just too far for them to reach Earth in any meaningful time, so don't worry too much. Unless they can travel the speed of light. Then you might worry.

Sisyphean

adj. – endless and fruitless (task)

Marking books endlessly, day after day, is a Sisyphean task.

Sisyphus was a Corinthian king who was punished for his deceit by Zeus and was made to roll a boulder up a hill in Hades, which would fall back down, and he would rinse and repeat.

goldilocks

adj. – not too extreme (i.e., not too hot, not too cold)

The goldilocks planet looks to be a perfect opportunity for life.

The Goldilocks Zone is an area in another solar system that is not too far from a sun nor too close so the temperature is just right for life to perhaps exist. The planets in other solar systems are called exoplanets.

fenestrated

adj. – having windows

The building's glass fenestration was an unusual style for the time period.

Defenestration is a much more interesting word – throwing out of a window. The Defenestration of Prague was when some people got thrown out of a window. They survived, but it started the Thirty Years War.

cabal

n. – a small group of conspirators or plotters

Unfortunately, the cabal looking to take over this place have no regard for the people who work in this building.

From the French "cabal" but also popularized as Charles II had five intriguing ministers with names whose initial letters spelled "cabal".

cavalcade

n. – a procession of people on horseback or in cars

The President's cavalcade drove slowly through the town.

More recently the suffix "-cade" had come to mean "a procession", as in "motorcade".

errant

adj. – erring or straying from the right course; wondering

"You will be punished for your errant ways, boy!"

Originally meaning "travelling, roving" but now meaning more off the beaten track.

compunction

n – distress, anxiety about an action or given result

He had no compunction about moving house to live in a new town.

I have no compunction about using the word "compunction". I love it. Good word.

titular

adj. – relating to or bearing a title

Daniel Radcliffe starred as the titular wizard Harry Potter in all of the films.

I deeply detest social distinction and snobbery, and in that lies my strong aversion to titular honours.
—Helen Clark

whicker

v. – to neigh or whinny; to snicker or stifle a laugh

The horse gave a nervous whicker; it was prone to whickering.

The origin is imitative or echoic, which means onomatopoeic, so this is supposedly the sound a horse makes.

jape

n., v. – joke, jest

He loved to joke and jape about.

Aah, the classic Monty Python "Jape Sketch" ("History of the Joke Sketch"). Worth a watch.

flimflam

n. – nonsense, foolishness; swindle, deception

There's lots of flimflam on the TV to distract the viewer away from the important things in life.

Possibly from Scandinavia and possibly echoic (onomatopoeic). Not much help there. Sorry.

razzle-dazzle

adj., n. – showy, flashy

The razzle-dazzle presentation that the teacher gave was full of technology and had the children completely engaged.

First seen in the "Clothier and Furnisher" magazine, Jan. 1889. So there you go. Those "scarfs of disjointed pattern" mentioned therein were obviously quite something.

cumbrous

adj. – cumbersome, difficult to handle due to weight/size

The cumbrous wooden carts were difficult for the oxen to pull along the rutted tracks.

I tried to look up a quotation to go here but they were all so cumbrous that I was unable to place one here for you.

Olympian

Adj. – majestic, divine, exalted

The man was Olympian in both size and the effort he put into his task. It was truly a great achievement.

The actual Mount Olympus, the fabled seat of the Greek gods, is only 2,917 metres (9,570 ft) tall. Not all that Olympian, really. Nice place though, by all accounts.

hapless

adj. – unfortunate, wretched

The hapless man stumbled out of the shop and put his foot straight into a deep puddle.

"Hap" is "luck, chance, fortune" from which we get "mishap", "happenchance*" and even "happen", meaning "to occur by hap".

ironfisted

adj. – ruthless, harsh; stingy

He ruled with an ironfisted ruthlessness that kept the people downtrodden.

Of course, he could have been ham-fisted. Either way, it doesn't solve the riddle of when, where and how the hyphen should be used.

mycology

n. – study of fungi

The biologist was an expert in mycology, particularly the study of edible mushrooms.

People who study me are mycologists because I'm such a…

obstreperous

adj. – unruly, boisterous, rowdy,

He was an obstreperous child, getting up to no good and into trouble at school.

"Stroppy" is possibly a slang version of "obstreperous". I mean, who needs four syllables when you could have two?

September 16th

gamify

v. – to adapt a task or something to be more game-like

Each drill at training had to be gamified to keep the children interested.

Gamification is important these days for keeping children interested in learning (making tasks like games) but even in app development for all sorts of things, as people love games and competing.

thew(s)

n. – muscle, muscular strength

Milo's own flabby form was pitted against the thews and sinews of John.

"Up, lad: thews that lie and cumber
Sunlit pallets never thrive;
Morns abed and daylight slumber
Were not meant for man alive."   (A.E. Housman)

Adonis

n. – a handsome young man

Johnny was nothing short of an Adonis, his muscular figure and chiselled looks were a pleasure to look upon.

No, it's true, honestly. Not just self-imposed blarney*.

profligate

adj. – wildly extravagant or wasteful, debauched

He was a profligate man, throwing many incredible parties for all of his friends.

Originally, it meant "overthrown, routed" from the Latin "profligatus" meaning "destroyed, ruined, corrupt, abandoned, dissolute" before taking on its newer meaning.

September 20th

sheeple

n. – people who follow the majority in opinion or matters

"Look at all the sheeple around you, being good little people and doing what they are told!"

"Meeple", on the other hand, are little playing pieces used in board games to represent people. The question we all want answering, though, is can you have sheeple meeple?

supernumerary

adj. – exceeding in regular number of

Jess grew a number of supernumerary teeth, some growing down from the roof of her mouth.

I have seen pictures of a whole roof of the mouth being filled with teeth. It makes me feel physically sick.

superlunary

adj. – situated above or beyond the moon, celestial

The spaceship left Earth's atmosphere to start its superlunary journey into the unknown.

Of course, I think it should be "superdairycheese", partly because I love cheese, but also because we all know what the moon is actually made of. I'm vegan now, so hey ho.

multitudinous

adj. – very numerous

There were multitudinous entries into the book.

Three hundred and sixty-five, to be accurate.

roughshod

adj. – of a horse with horseshoes to prevent sliding

The government ran roughshod over the rights of its people.

Nothing to do with "shoddy", whose etymology (word history) is related to both Yorkshire and the American Civil War. Look it up. Be an active reader.

palindrome

n. – a word or phrase that reads the same backwards and forwards

"Able was I, ere I saw Elba."

And "Snug & raw was I ere I saw war & guns." The first pertaining to Napoleon and both appearing in a U.S. periodical called "Gazette of the Union" in 1848, written by "J.T.R.".

murdrum

n. - the killing of a human being in a secret manner

King Richard confirmed the Templars' land holdings and granted them immunity from all pleas and from murdrum.

Of course, the reason that this word is on this page should be obvious…

rancorous

n. – a feeling of bitterness, hostility, spite

Mr Schmidt was a rancorous old man: always unhappy and rude.

Originally from the Latin "rancere" meaning "to stink" from which we get the word "rancid". Another great word.

dotard

n. – confused or foolish person (esp. through old age)

The poor dotard wanted to be the town mayor but he had little chance.

The root word is "dote" from which we also get the now-obsolete word "doddypoll" meaning "stupid person". Let's get that word back into usage. I know I could use it a lot.

scullion

n. – a mean or despicable person; a kitchen servant

He started life out as a scullion but soon rose through the ranks at the house.

"Away, you scullion! you rampallian! you fustilarian! I'll tickle your catastrophe."
— William Shakespeare, Henry IV, Part 2

manumission

n. – the act of freeing or being freed from slavery

Rather than encouraging his countrymen to liberate their slaves, he opposed such manumission.

Let's hope this is a thing of the past and that it stays that way. At least, it *should* be a thing of the past.

cacophony

n. – harsh or discordant sound, jarring noise

The cacophony from inside the hall was enough to make his ears bleed.

Yes, the prefix actually comes from "kaka-" or "kakka-", the Proto-Indo-European root meaning "to defecate". That's how bad the sound is.

Land of Nod

n. - imaginary land of sleep

And off she finally went to the Land of Nod.

First used in 1738 by Jonathan Swift (1667-1745) in the very long-titled *A Complete Collection of Genteel and Ingenious Conversation, according to the Most Polite Mode and Method now used at Court, and in the Best Companies of England.*

homily

n. – a moralizing sermon or speech

The priest thankfully gave a brief homily.

Also connected are homilist, homiletic and homiliary. Actually, one of those isn't a real word. But which one?

ripsnorter

n. – person or thing that is forceful, exciting, wild; a humdinger*

"That was a real ripsnorter of a ride! This theme park is awesome."

First used in 1840 by whacking "rip" and "snort" together. I guess that's how you make words.

humdinger

n. – something impressive, exciting enjoyable; a ripsnorter*

Sam didn't think that ride was a real humdinger. He had such high expectations for theme parks.

First used in 1883 by possibly whacking "hum" and "dinger" together. I guess that's how you make words.

inculcate

v. – to impress upon someone by forceful repetition

I tried to inculcate a sense of politeness into my children.

Don't forget your Ps and Qs. Don't forget your Ps and Qs. Don't forget your Ps and Qs. Don't forget your Ps and Qs. Don't forget your Ps and Qs. Don't forget your Ps and Qs.

gerund

n. – noun formed from -ing ending verb

The singing boys liked **singing**.

Here, the act of singing is a verb used as a noun. People wrongly think words ending in "-ing" are automatically verbs. No, it depends upon the function of the word. Here, the act of singing is a thing, a noun.

gerundive

n. – an adjective formed from a verb

The **singing** *boys liked singing.*

Here, singing is being used to describe the boys, so it is an adjective. See how many gerunds and gerundives you use today. You might not use this but it's good to know, eh?

boondoggle

n. – futile, unnecessary task

Building the bridge was a complete boondoggle – overdue, over budget and nobody needed it.

Lovely sounding word, but of unknown origin. I wonder if people will say this book is a boondoggle.

meme

n. – an idea or social behaviour; image or video spread on the internet

"You've got to see this meme – it's hilarious. I'll share it with you now."

Any idea that passes on and persists is a meme. Folding the end sheet of toilet paper in hotel bathrooms is a meme that remains because it has some use. I think it has some use.

metanoia

n. – a fundamental change in character or outlook

I experienced a profound metanoia and changed my ways.

"Meta-" has three meanings: 1) higher, beyond; 2) after, behind, among, between; 3) changed, altered. So, lots of opportunity for "meta-" words. How many can you think of?

bamboozle

v. – to cheat, mislead; confuse

"You really bamboozled me with that riddle."

One of the saddest lessons of history is this: If we've been bamboozled long enough, we tend to reject any evidence of the bamboozle. We're no longer interested in finding out the truth. The bamboozle has captured us. —Carl Sagan

gargantuan

adj. – huge, massive

The gargantuan building stood over them like a hulking monster.

From Rabelais' novels from the 1590s, named after *Gargantua*, a voracious* giant.

kludge

n. – a clumsy or unsophisticated solution that ends up working

The IT system they constructed was a real kludge, but it got the job done.

Some could say the same about this book. Author Jackson W. Granholm defined his own word as an "ill-assorted collection of poorly-matching parts, forming a distressing whole".

inexorable

adj. – not able to be persuaded; relentless

Is the inexorable rise of technology in our society a worry or a good thing?

Well, is it? Discuss this today with someone.

voracious

adj. – greedy in eating; eager

The tiger had a voracious appetite.

Unlucky, since the circus artist had his head in its mouth.

quotidian

adj. – daily; everyday or usual

The battles of quotidian existence are getting your children to eat well, do their homework and brush their teeth.

Get dressed on time, say their Ps and Qs, treat others with respect, try their hardest in all they do, be kind, speak kindly… Complete the list. Not a lot to ask, really.

kibosh

v. – to put a stop to

The car broke down, putting a kibosh on the day trip.

Earliest use is in Dickens, but it could come from the Irish "caip bháis" or "caipín báis" meaning "cap of death", said to be the black cap a judge would don when pronouncing a death sentence.

slush fund

n. – money collected to buy luxuries (or pay for illegal political/business activities)

The company has a slush fund to pay for things like that.

"Slush fund" is from an earlier sense of slush: "refuse fat; the money from the sale of a ship's slush was shared among the officers. First attested in 1839.

oxymoron

n. – a figure of speech in which opposite terms are used together

Alone together, we can act naturally, though clearly confused, in this bittersweet deafening silence.

How oxymoronic can you be?

gadfly

n. – a constantly irritating person

The Scout leader was something of a gadfly, always nagging and annoying the troop.

A plague of gadflies was supposed to be one of the plagues of Egypt. What's worse, a plague of irritating humans or a plague of cattle-biting insects?

atrophy

n., v. – wasting away, degeneration (usually of an organ)

In the same way that he had atrophy of the brain, sadly his personality had also started to atrophy.

I have multiple sclerosis and so, no doubt, cerebral (brain) atrophy. There is no way I see it as a trophy, though.

gaslight

v. – to manipulate someone by constantly giving them false information so they doubt their sanity

"Don't gaslight me into thinking there is actually a ghost in here!"

From Patrick Hamilton's 1938 play *Gas Light*, in which a husband tries to drive his wife insane by falsely claiming that the gaslight in their home is not becoming dimmer.

chagrin

n. – feeling of annoyance

Much to my chagrin, there is no decent restaurant open.

Physical pain is easily forgotten, but a moral chagrin lasts indefinitely.
—Santiago Ramon y Cajal

dervish

n. – a member of a Muslim religious group that sometimes practice whirling and chanting

Whirling like a dervish, she spun around the dancefloor.

Jalal ad-Din Muhammad Rumi was a Persian poet, an Islamic dervish who said: "Yesterday I was clever, so I wanted to change the world. Today I am wise, so I am changing myself."

eke

v. – to increase, lengthen

You can't eke out a living do that all day! It pays a pittance.

A northern English and East Midland variant of an Old English word from a Proto-Germanic word from the Proto-Indo-European word "aug" meaning "to increase". That's history for you.

debunk

v. – to disprove or expose false claims

He spent time debunking various conspiracy theories.

Take your pick: the moon landing was faked, the Loch Ness Monster, lizardmen in human costumes run the US government, UFOs are kept in Roswell, there is a mind-control lab in Alaska, President JFK was killed by...?

gung-ho

adj. – extremely enthusiastic; keen to participate (esp. in military combat)

He was very gung-ho about the changes he wanted to make for the team, making them straight away and with little thought of their feelings.

From World War II and US troops in the Pacific, from the Chinese "kung ho" meaning "to work together".

bugbear

n. – a thing that causes obsessive fear or anxiety

Not tucking your chair in after getting up from the table is a real bugbear of mine.

Possibly from Old Welsh "bwg" meaning "goblin"; in Medieval England, the bugbear was a creepy bear that lurked in the woods scaring children. Nice.

conflate

v. – to confuse two things together

"You are conflating working hard with being a good, moral person, when these are two separate things."

I find this word incredibly useful when I write my more geeky, philosophical things as so many people conflate one idea with another.

mediocracy

n. – government or rule by mediocre person or group

The school was run under a mediocracy with no pupil or staff member pushed to their potential.

Here are some more free ones for you: theocracy, autocracy, democracy, nondemocracy, technocracy, aristocracy, meritocracy, slavocracy, kleptocracy, pantisocracy, adhocracy.

swashbuckler

n. – a swaggering, flamboyant adventurer

I wonder whether Errol Flynn was the ultimate movie swashbuckler.

From the 1550s, meaning "blustering, swaggering fighting man", from "swash" meaning "fall of a blow" + "buckler", "shield". Originally seems to have been "one who makes menacing noises by striking his or an opponent's shield".

incandescent

n. – red- or white-hot; extremely angry

She was incandescent with rage, though you couldn't tell.

"Slice a pear and you will find that its flesh is incandescent white. It glows with inner light. Those who carry a knife and a pear are never afraid of the dark."
—Yann Martel, Beatrice and Virgil

invective

n. – vehement*, abusive accusation or language

Paul's constant invective made for an unhealthy relationship.

Invective may be a sharp weapon, but overuse blunts its edge. Even when the denunciation is just and true it is an error of art to indulge it too long.
—John Tyndall

reticent

adj. – restrained, quiet, reluctant

She was reticent to start her work before 5pm.

I'm not sure why one needs to add "before 5pm"…

repudiate

v. – to reject, refuse to acknowledge

The lawyer easily repudiated the claims of his opponent.

Everyone admits that "the truth hurts" but no one applies this adage to himself — and as soon as it begins to hurt us, we quickly repudiate it and call it a lie.
—Sydney J. Harris

unctuous

adj. – oily, greasy; smug or smooth in manner

First, they listened to an unctuous grace from Friar Tuck, and then Robin lifted high a tankard of ale.

Is stealing always bad? What if you steal from the rich to give to the poor? Or some bread to feed your starving family? What makes good *good* or bad *bad*?

ignominious

adj. – despicable; degrading or shameful

He endured terrible and ignominious tortures in the dungeon.

Have you ever done something that could be described as "ignominious"? Do you regret it?

argy-bargy

n. – argument or squabble

"There was a bit of argy-bargy when people started ignoring the queueing system. It was quite the hullabaloo*!"

From "argle-bargle", with "argle" meaning "to argue obstinately*", an evolution of "argue".

hurly-burly

n. – turmoil, confusion, commotion

In the hurly-burly of the argy-bargy* that came from the hoi-polloi* who were scattered pell-mell* about the deck, you couldn't hear yourself think.

There are so many brilliant rhyming compounds that you could almost do a Word of the Day book on them! That said, I don't want to bore you with claptrap and gibble-gabble.

hoity-toity

adj. – arrogant, condescending

The assistants in the hoity-toity shop refused to serve her because they thought she looked homeless.

Originally more to do with "riotous behaviour" from an earlier "highty tighty". Perhaps it came to mean "haughty*" because it sounded similar.

happenchance

n. – fluke, coincidence

It was complete happenchance that they met again in the same shop.

Or happenstance? You say tomato, I say tomato.

taupe

adj. – brownish-grey colour

She wore a taupe skirt to attract as little attention as possible.

Colour synonyms: camel, cream, khaki, off-white, tan, biscuit, buff, ecru, fawn*, mushroom, neutral, oatmeal, sand, café au lait.

vexatious

adj. – full of or causing annoyance, distress

He gets a bit vexatious when you start questioning him.

As I always tell people, question everything, apart from what I say. That is sacrosanct. Ooh, good word. How did that not end up in here? Well, it's here now.

fetid

adj. – having stale, nauseating smell (of decay)

Opening the bag with the crow's carcass within, she was assaulted with a fetid smell.

Which word do you think is the strongest? Noxious, putrid, revolting, smelly, stinking, stinky, corrupt, fusty, gross, malodorous, offensive, rank, reeking, repugnant, or repulsive?

narcissistic

n. – exceptionally interested in or admiring of oneself

He was so narcissistic that every decision he made was only concerned with how he would look to everyone else and not whether it was right.

Narcissus was a handsome young Greek hunter, admired by many but showing contempt. The goddess of revenge led him to a pool where he fell in love with his own reflection. He eventually realised and committed suicide in despair.

pulchritude

n. – beauty

She was a woman of great pulchritude.

Again, another word that sounds opposite to what it means. Such an ugly sounding word!

stolid

adj. – showing little emotion or interest

Alfie was a stolid man; giving little away and hard to get on with.

When success follows you, be stolid otherwise you'll get spoiled.
—Sudithi

homunculus

n. – a miniature person

A little, green homunculus fell from the branch and landed in front of me.

Do we have a homunculus living in our brains, watching everything on a tiny, internal cinema screen, making decisions and sending out commands? No. No, we don't.

de rigueur

adj. – required by etiquette; fashionable

It is now de rigueuer for children to have their own YouTube channels.

Everything today seems to be required to be seen on a device or to be recorded. We can't just enjoy something once, in a fleeting moment. It must be recorded and placed online, for everyone. Forever. For why?

behemoth

n. – anything huge or powerful

The man was a veritable behemoth, towering over everyone else.

A huge biblical beast, it probably came from the Egyptian "pehemau", a "water-ox" – the name for a hippopotamus. I mean, they're *pretty* big…

leviathan

n. – anything huge or powerful

Like a hulking leviathan, he stood menacingly at the door.

This biblical beast was a water-based (maybe crocodilic) monster, and the word is of unknown origin (perhaps Hebrew or Arabic). I don't think "crocodilic" is a word but it should be.

poppycock

n. – foolish talk, nonsense

"What a load of poppycock. Absolute rubbish."

Probably from Dutch, with "pappekak": "pappe" meaning "soft food" and "kak" meaning, yup, "dung". So, soft food dung. Yum yum. Those crazy Dutch people, eh!

probity

n. – uprightness, of high moral behaviour or standard

He had unswerving probity, serving in his position with great integrity.

Take from a man his reputation for probity, and the more shrewd and clever he is, the more hated and mistrusted he becomes.
— Marcus Tullius Cicero

namby-pamby

adj. – weak, feeble, spineless

Too many countries have a namby-pamby attitude to the environment.

You'd be surprised. Girls like sensitive, namby-pamby guys.
—Lizzy Caplan
Phew, there's hope for us, yet. Right, now to finish my fifty press-ups.

replete

adj. – to be full of, supplied with

The old box came replete with all its contents and even the instructions.

Replete. Complete. What's the difference? That's today's homework.

saccharine

adj. – excessively sweet

The movie was saccharine, with a very typical happy ending.

According to 2008 Guinness World Records, thaumatin (also known as talin) is the sweetest known substance. It is 1,600 times as sweet as sucrose. I always say "sweet as a nut" but they aren't even that sweet. Not like thaumatin, anyway.

skullduggery

n. – underhand dealing, trickery, dishonest behaviour

He was aware of his friend's general skullduggery but he still liked him.

One "l" or two? One of the most important questions of our age. Tomato, tomato.

resplendent

adj. – having a brilliant, dazzling, splendid appearance

The resplendent room was the most decorated in the palace.

The richest man in history is Mansa Musa, the king of Timbuktu, who lived between 1280 and 1337. Timbuktu was the largest producer of gold when it was in huge demand. It is thought he was worth $400 billion in today's money.

bombastic

adj. – inflated, pretentious, high-sounding

The speech was over-the-top and too bombastic for the audience.

What has a writer to be bombastic about? Whatever good a man may write is the consequence of accident, luck, or surprise, and nobody is more surprised than an honest writer when he makes a good phrase or says something truthful.
—Edward Dahlberg

foment

v. – to encourage, instigate, stir up

The staff were asked to foment excitement amongst the children ready for the big day.

Abigail Adams, an early advocate of women's rights, said: "If particular care and attention is not paid to the Ladies we are determined to foment a Rebellion…"

incorrigible

adj. – beyond correction or reform

Jack's behaviour in class was incorrigible. Nothing seemed to work to help him and the teacher manage his outbursts.

I have children whose behaviour *out* of class is also incorrigible. Oh, the joys of parenthood.

reprehensible

adj. – bad behaviour, person or idea open to criticism

The fact that they didn't give us an apology was reprehensible.

I wonder if there are far more words for bad behaviour and negative emotions than positive ones.

hullaballoo

n. – a loud noise or commotion

The group caused quite a hullaballoo about not having enough food.

Originally "hollo bollo" with many variations, including the Americanism "hellabaloo". "Hollo" comes from "hello", which became a popular greeting after the advent of the telephone.

harbinger

n. – a person who announces or indicates the approach of something

Like a harbinger of doom, she brought very bad news.

At one time, the word meant "innkeeper", though I hardly think an innkeeper bringing a tankard of ale to a customer is a harbinger of doom.

capitulate

v. – to surrender, stop resisting

After they went one goal down, the team utterly capitulated.

Hiroo Onoda refused to surrender after the Second World War, surviving in the Philippines forests and hills from 1945 until 1974. However, lesser-known Teruo Nakamura survived even longer on an Indonesian island until later the same year.

bellwether

n. – an indicator of trends

I think that Jason is a real bellwether for what's cool in the music industry.

It also means leader and comes from when a lead sheep would carry a bell ("belle", with "whether" being a male sheep).

recidivism

n. – the tendency to go back into crime

The key to measuring the success of prisons is to measure the recidivism rates – how many prisoners go back into a life of crime when released?

Should prisons be harsh and punishing, or should they give you the skills to become a better person? Norway takes the latter approach and has around only a 20% recidivism rate.

sagacious

adj. – intelligent, wise

The old teacher was a sagacious woman who knew exactly how to handle the most difficult children.

Sagacity is another great word (from the Latin "keenness of perception"). You would be wise to agree with me.

foursquare

adj. – unyielding, firm; honest

I have been foursquare in my support of greater human rights.

Square gets a lot more words and phrases than triangle. I think the world is trianglist.

exculpate

v. – to free from blame

"Don't think you have exculpated yourself from this matter, young man!"

Exculpatory is also a lovely sounding word. "Culpa" is Latin for "blame", from where we get the phrase "mea culpa" – I am to blame.

behoove

v. – to be necessary, proper, worthwhile (to do)

It would behoove you to find out where you are going before setting off!

It would certainly behoove you to behave around a beehive.

malinger

v. – to shirk; pretend to be ill to escape work

"First, you told me that your dog ate your homework and then you claim you were ill when I think you were malingering."

A child swore blind to me once that a dog actually did eat his homework. I believed him, too.

ersatz

adj. – to be made in imitation of something genuine

The gluten-free ersatz version of the farmhouse loaf was well received.

During WWII, Han Van Meegeren sold what was believed to be an original Vermeer to Field Marshall Goering. It turns out he painted over sixteen paintings so well, he made over $30 million in today's money. He escaped a death penalty. Just.

effulgent

adj. - radiant

As she stood at the sun-drenched window, she glowed with divinely effulgent splendour.

Do not confuse this word with effluent. That would be bad.

accentuate

v. – to stress or emphasise

His well-weathered face accentuated his age.

It's almost Christmas. Here are some "-uate" words for free. Fluctuate, punctuate, attenuate, inadequate, perpetuate, effectuate, insinuate, eventuate, habituate, graduate, extenuate, You're welcome.

highfalutin

adj. – pompous, pretentious

"You won't convince me with your highfalutin ideas and language!"

Whether you put an apostrophe at the end or not, we still don't know exactly where the word came from. I like it, though. Makes me want to say "rootin' tootin'" ("noisy, rambunctious").

iridescent

adj. – having softly shifting changes of colour

The butterfly's wings dazzled with their iridescent brilliance.

While a human eye has 3 photoreceptors (red, green, blue), a mantis shrimp has 12-16 per eye: it can see polarised and UV light. It can perceive depth with one eye (where we need two). In comparison, we're rubbish. Meh, we've got cinemas.

redolent

adj. – reminiscent, suggestive of

The smell of the pie was redolent of his childhood, of his grandmother's house particularly.

From the Latin meaning "emit a scent" or "diffuse an odour". The smell of cut grass in the summer is always one that gets me.

scarper

v. – to depart in haste, run away

The boys bolted out of the classroom and scarpered.

Probably from Italian "scappare" meaning "to escape" and influenced by rhyming slang Scapa Flow "go". I regularly use "You're having a bubble bath" for "laugh".

zeitgeist

n. – spirit of the age, a trend of thought

His song captured the zeitgeist of the time and his neighbourhood.

What three things sum up the zeitgeist of your youth (bearing in mind that could be right now!)?

troglodyte

n. – cave-dweller; recluse; someone who lives primitively

"Why don't you have a mobile phone? You're such a troglodyte!"

From the Latin and Greek meaning "one who creeps into holes". Not to be confused with trolls, who live under bridges.

fait accompli

n. – something already done or unchangeable

Although there were four people going for the job, the choice was a fait accompli: Giselle had it in the bag.

Fate is fait accompli.
— Messaoud Mohammed

parsimonious

adj. – miserly; sparing

A far more parsimonious explanation is: you're ignorant.

Harsh, but to the point. There is something called Ockham's Razor that says if two theories do the same job, then the simplest one is preferable. I have been parsimonious with my explanation of it here…

avuncular

adj. – friendly, helpful; jolly

Anika was an avuncular old woman, always smiling and helping.

Oddly enough, "avuncular" is not a very jolly-sounding word.

phlegmatic

adj. – not easily excited, calm amid turmoil

Given the panicked pandemonium going on in the kitchen around Grandpa Jim, he was surprisingly phlegmatic.

Christmas lunch, eh! So much to do, so little time to do it AND open presents AND have fun.

lachrymose

adj. – given to crying easily

He was a lachrymose young lad, never far from a good cry.

Pet owners often claim that dogs cry, and Darwin thought that monkeys and elephants cried, but nowadays scientists think that only humans cry, though other animals do show emotions.

assiduous

adj. – hard-working, persevering

As an assiduous man, he was back to work as soon after Christmas as possible.

As a deciduous man, his hair fell out from all the stress. But it grew back again, so all was well.

supercilious

adj. – displaying indifference, arrogant pride

He was supercilious to think in assuming he would win the trophy without even trying hard. He failed.

The sweaty players in the game of life always have more fun than the supercilious spectators.
—William Feather

cantankerous

adj. – bad-tempered, quarrelsome

The cantankerous old man raised his fists to the air and wandered off.

He was evidently annoyed that he had come to the end of his "Word of the Day" book. He shouldn't worry. There are plenty more words out there, waiting to be savoured. Or he could reuse some of the ones he has learnt.

denouement

n. – the final outcome, solution (in a play, book etc.)

The bittersweet denouement to her holiday meant she had some sad farewells to make.

I wonder what the greatest denouement is that you have experienced to any movie or book you have read or watched?

supplementary

adj. – additional, ancillary

The readers expected some supplementary entries at the end of the book.

Yeah, no. That's enough for now. You can always start again at the beginning. Reignite, reawaken, rekindle, relight renew, restart, restore, revive.

About the author

Johnny Pearce is a teacher and author who has written a number of different books on a number of different topics. His most recent foray into the world of fiction was a children's and young adult fiction book, *The Curse of the Maya*. Check it out: it's really good! He lives in Hampshire with his partner and twin boys. The trials and tribulations of helping to bring twins into the world led him to write the book *Twins: A Survival Guide for Dads*. Also a thoroughly good book. Well, he thinks so, anyway.

Milton Keynes UK
Ingram Content Group UK Ltd.
UKHW020922271223
434976UK00014B/530